SOMETIMES MOON

BY Carole Lexa Schaefer ○ ILLUSTRATED BY Pierr Morgan

CROWN PUBLISHERS, INC. ♛ NEW YORK

One night,
at a full moon family picnic,
while waiting for Moon to come up,

Grandpapa says,
"The moon waxes and wanes,
wanes and waxes.
Did you know?"

I know.

I always look out for Moon.

Sometimes it hides—like me.

I hide behind the blowing curtains.

Papa comes looking for me.

"Selene . . . Selie," he calls.
"I know you are there.
Come on out!"

I talk like that to Hiding Moon.
I point at the sky and holler,
"I know you are up there
behind the shadows.
Come on out!"
It takes a while,
but Moon *does* come out—

sometimes as thin and silver as
Grandpapa's dory boat out in the bay.

Grandpapa mends nets for catching fish.

With my fingers,
I make crisscross lines
on Dory Boat Moon.
"Here's a net for you," I say,
"so *your* fish won't jump out
and splash back in the water."

Sometimes Moon is a half circle
with a dip in the middle —
like Mama's knitting basket.

Mama pulls yarn out of her basket.
She knits and knits the yarn together
to make a woolly sweater for me.

I squiggle yarn lines
inside Moon.
"Big Basket Moon,
your yarn is as light
as spiderweb strings," I say.
"And enough to keep Mama knitting
for a long, long time."

Sometimes Moon is kind of round and chubby—
like Baby Nico's cheeks.

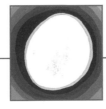

Nico sleeps in a cradle
that I can rock with my feet.

I draw a rocking cradle
under Moon in the sky.
"Rock-a-bye, loo loo lee,"
I sing for Baby Nico—
and for Cheeky Moon.

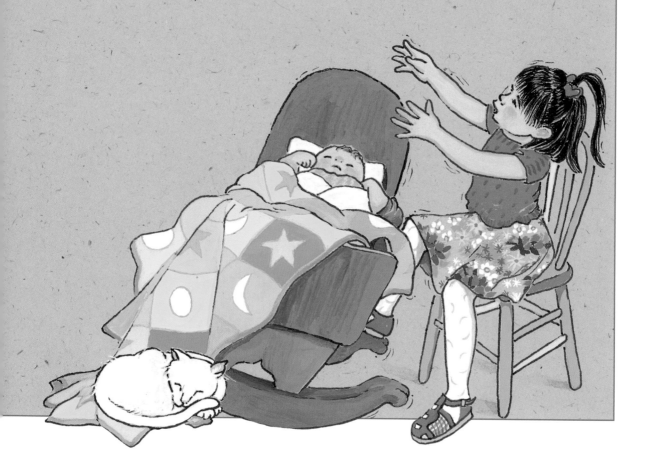

At the full moon family picnic,
while waiting for Moon to come up,
Grandpapa says, "The moon waxes and wanes,
wanes and waxes. Did you know?"

Grandmama says,
"He means it grows and shrinks.
And shrinks and grows."

"I know," I say.
I make moons in the sand.
Grandmama looks at them.
"Aha," she says, and wraps her arms
in a circle around me.
"See here what I'm holding?
Something bright that keeps on growing.
It's my own Queen of the Moon—
Selene!"

Then
    the
        Sometimes Full Moon
           comes up,
as shiny and round
as a piece of Queen Selene's gold.
I raise my arms up high
and make a circle, too.
"Look," I say. "See what *I'm* holding?"

How the Moon Wanes and Waxes

Our Earth's moon is shaped like a ball. It goes around and around Earth in a circular path we call an orbit. Sunlight brightens the half of the moon that faces the sun. The half of the moon turned away from the sun is dark. When we see the fully lighted half of the moon, we call it the full moon. But as the moon travels around our Earth, we usually see only part of the lighted side, because even though the lighted half faces the sun, it doesn't always face Earth.

As the moon orbits around us, we see less and less of its lighted half. This makes the moon look as though it is changing shape, as if it is shrinking — *waning* — from full, to three-quarters, to half, to a crescent moon. But the moon is still a ball, with less and less of its lighted side facing Earth, until its dark side is turned toward us. Since all we see of it now is the dark side, it seems as if our moon has disappeared. We call this the new moon.

But the moon doesn't really disappear. It continues in its orbit, and soon we can see a sliver of the side lit by the sun. Then it seems to change shape again as we see more of the lighted side, growing bigger and bigger — *waxing* — from crescent, to half, to three-quarters, until, once more, we see the full moon.

It takes a little over 27 days for the moon to travel around Earth and to go through all of these changes. We call the changes the phases of the moon.

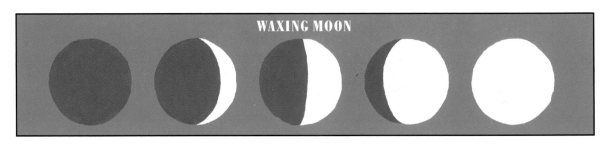

WAXING MOON

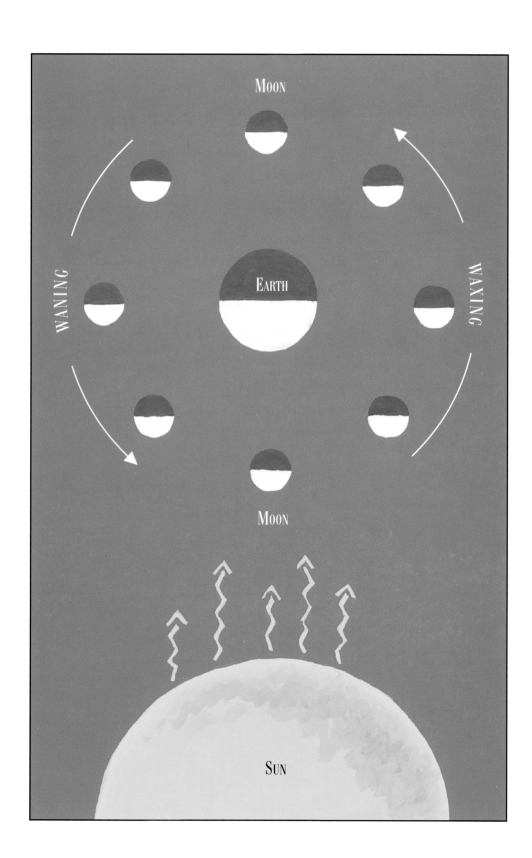

To all our friends on the island of Kefalloniá,
and especially to Thalia & Terry, and Sheila & Pete

—C. L. S. & P. M.

The art was done with Winsor Newton gouache on 80-lb.,
100%-recycled "Oatmeal" Speckle-tone paper from France.

Text copyright © 1999 by Carole Lexa Schaefer
Illustrations copyright © 1999 by Pierr Morgan

Published by Crown Publishers, Inc., a Random House company, 201 East 50th Street, New York, NY 10022

CROWN is a trademark of Crown Publishers, Inc.

www.randomhouse.com/kids

Library of Congress Cataloging-in-Publication Data
Schaefer, Carole Lexa.
Sometimes moon / by Carole Lexa Schaefer ; illustrated by Pierr Morgan.
p.   cm.
Summary: A girl describes how sometimes she sees the changing moon as thin and silver like
Grandpapa's dory boat, sometimes as a half circle like Mama's knitting basket, and sometimes round
and chubby like the baby's cheeks.
[1. Moon—Phases—Fiction.]   I. Morgan, Pierr, ill.   II. Title.
PZ7.S3315So   1999
[E]—dc21   97-46666

ISBN 0-517-70980-5 (trade)
ISBN 0-517-70981-3 (lib. bdg.)

Printed in Singapore
10 9 8 7 6 5 4 3 2 1

First Edition